UNASHAMEDLY BLACK AND UNAPOLOGETICALLY CHRISTIAN

Volume I

UNASHAMEDLY BLACK AND UNAPOLOGETICALLY
CHRISTIAN

A POETIC AFFIRMATION OF CULTURAL
IDENTITY AND DIVINE SPIRITUALITY

by
Charles L. Hinsley
Volume I

LINGUISTIC FREEDOM PUBLICATIONS, LLC
Jamestown, North Carolina

Unashamedly Black and Unapologetically Christian:
A Poetic Affirmation of Cultural Identity and Divine Spirituality
Volume I

Copyright © 2022 Charles L. Hinsley

All rights reserved. No portion of this book may be reproduced mechanically, electronically, or by any other means, including photocopying, without written permission from the publisher. It is illegal to copy this book, post it to a website, or distribute it by any other means without permission from the publisher.

Published by Linguistic Freedom Publications, LLC
Jamestown, North Carolina
linguisticfreedompublications@gmail.com

Edited by Lonnell Johnson

Cover design by Randy Kassebaum
Interior design by Imagine!® Studios, www.ArtsImagine.com

Interior illustrations by Abdul Wahab Hashmi
Interior photographs by Leigh Bedokis

"The Door of No Return" photograph by Chris Miller.
Praying hand image by Nathan Dumlao on Unsplash.
Used by permission.

Scripture quotations taken from the The Holy Bible, King James Version.

ISBN: 978-0-9895873-3-4 (Volume I)
ISBN: 978-0-9895873-4-1 (Volume II)

Library of Congress Control Number: 2022947198

First Linguistic Freedom Publications, LLC printing: October 2022

TABLE OF CONTENTS

Acknowledgments xi
Foreword xiii
About the Author xx
Water Our Roots xxii
The Preamble xxiv
The Prelude xxv
The Image of God xxvii

CHAPTER ONE
PRIDE / 1

Homeland 2
African American Black Negro Child 4
Freedom 6
Equilibrium 8
Fly in the Buttermilk 10
My Poems, My People 12
The Door of NO Return 14

CHAPTER TWO
SPIRITUAL CONSCIOUSNESS / 17

The Light of Day 18
(The Parenthesis of Life) 21
Perpendicular Focus 24
Proof 26
Divine Proclamation 33

CHAPTER THREE
NEGRO TALK / 37

Cotton Club Sister 38
A Street Corner Chess Game 40
Brother Ray 42
Sister 'Trish 45
Bay-Bay Kids and Negroes 47
Nigga Street 50
Nine-Eleven, 2001 52

CHAPTER FOUR
NOTIONS OF LIFE / 55

Where There's a Will, There's a Way 56
Intimations of the Essentials 58
Speak to My Heart 61
Collateral Impact 63
To Be 65
Thought Collector 67
Tears of the Son 69

CHAPTER FIVE
SILHOUETTE SOLILOQUY, A JAZZ FINALE / 71

Misty Blue 72
Misty Blue (Pictorial) 73
Contemplation of Jazz (Pictorial) 74
Incandescent Sound 75
My Musical Heritage 76
Solo Performance (Pictorial) 77

ACKNOWLEDGMENTS

First and foremost, I give thanks and honor to my Heavenly Father for HIS mercy, grace, and unconditional love given unto me through the blood and resurrection of HIS son, Jesus Christ.

To my wife Lori, my son Nicholas, my daughters Olivia, and Annika. You are the centerpiece of my world, and I am immensely rich because of your love. I am forever thankful to you, and I love you dearly. To my siblings, Gail, Jimmy, Gwen, Reggie, Teresa, and Kemperal. The DNA that binds us together is a heavenly gift that I cherish deeply. I love you guys very much. To my extended relatives, my in-laws, as well as, all my friends, and the African Diaspora, I thank you from the bottom of my heart for your support. Your genuine kindness combined with the richness of your love has given immeasurable meaning to my life, and it has been the inspiration for many of the thoughts I have expressed in this book.

To Reverend Dr. Jeremiah A. Wright, Jr., Pastor Emeritus of Trinity United Church of Christ in Chicago, Illinois. I offer a deep heartfelt thanks to you, Sir, for honoring me with the permission to use your church's motto for the title of my book. Granting me this privilege gave life to my dream and added confirmation to my soul to express the beliefs of our cultural pride in my own way and unapologetically. But additionally, I thank you for your gracious honor in writing the Foreword for my book. Your pastor-teacher gift added a distinct cultural and spiritual perspective to the meaning of my book that only a bold Black man of God could articulate. I thank you deeply for our friendship and the spiritual enlightenment you have provided me for over thirty years through your sermonic teachings of God's word.

To Abdul Wahab Hashmi, I thank you for supporting my book project with your artistic drawings. They added a complimentary flavor to the expression of my thoughts, and your skillful talent and intuitive insight added a visual perspective to my words that gives my book a one-of-a-kind appeal.

To Randy Kassebaum, I thank you immensely for your creative ingenuity in designing my book cover. Your visionary mind is simply extraordinary, and I benefited greatly from your talent. Thank you, my man!

To Chris Miller, I thank you for allowing me to use your photograph of The Door of No Return to accompany my poem of the same title. Your photograph provided a completely different poetic meaning to my words, and I am forever grateful for your kindness.

To Meredith Corporation and Getty Images for granting me permission to use the front cover of one of their *Life* magazine publications. Your image captured an indelible moment in the mind's eye of this nation's history known as Bloody Sunday, and it added immense context to my poem titled, "Walking With the Wind" honoring Congressman John Lewis and the countless other freedom fighters who have put their lives on the line to preserve our civil rights.

And, to Leigh Bedokis, I thank you for your photographic skills in creating my silhouette pictorials. Your assistance allowed me to add a unique presentation to my book.

FOREWORD

In 1969, I was a Research Assistant for the Fund for Theological Education (FTE). I was a student along with Bishop McKinley Young of the African Methodist Episcopal Church and Dr. Homer Ashby, the head of the Pastoral Care Department of McCormick Theological Seminary in Chicago. We were Ph.D. students at the Divinity School of the University of Chicago, and we were hired by the FTE to do research that would bless the lives of future seminarians and help seminaries accredited by the FTE to change their focus in the wake of the murder of Rev. Dr. Martin Luther King, Jr.

The two foci of our research were as follows: First, we were to gather from the Moorland-Spingarn Collection at Howard University, the libraries of Fisk University, and the Schomburg Collection in New York all of the written materials between them we could find about the Black Church.

We were assigned to compile a bibliography of Black Church Studies in 1969. Our primary sites for compiling that bibliography were those three locations.

The second focus of our research was to interview every African American pastor in the Chicago Metropolitan area who had attended or graduated from an FTE accredited seminary. The primary question of those interviews was to find out whether FTE seminaries had prepared them to work in the Black Church.

We were to interview pastors, preachers, seminary professors, pastoral counselors, hospital chaplains, college chaplains, prison chaplains, denominational mission staff, and persons doing ministry in multi-church staff positions. We interviewed Baptists, Methodists, Presbyterians, Lutherans, Anglicans, Unitarians, Pentecostal, and non-denominational clergy. The only criterion we had to adhere to was that they were to be graduates of FTE accredited seminaries.

While interviewing Dr. Reuben Sheares, a staff person working on inner-city ministries for the Chicago missionary arm of the United Church of Christ, the Community Renewal Society, Dr. Sheares pointed out that James Cone and Albert Cleage, Gayraud Wilmore, and Charles Long were black scholars and seminary professors writing to a new generation of persons preparing for work in theological education and in the Black Church. They were also writing about, writing to, and writing for a generation of Black persons who were different from the products of "the Negro Church" with which E. Franklin Frazier and Carter G. Woodson were familiar.

Following the murder of Dr. King and the urban unrest that sprung up from these tragic events, there emerged a new breed of Negros. He played upon what the title of Alain Locke's book, **The New Negro**, suggested by pointing out that the generation emerging in the late 60s were no longer Negroes. They were Black!

He characterized that generation (my generation) as the generation of believers who were "Unashamedly Black and unapologetically Christian."

Dr. Sheares, incidentally, was the Interim Pastor of Trinity United Church of Christ where I served for thirty-six years. He took that well-articulated term to the Trinity Church in 1971, and our congregation adopted it as our motto during his tenure as Interim Pastor.

When I pushed Dr. Sheares to say more about that term and what it meant, he said he coined that term because in his generation, Negroes had argued about whether to be called African, African American, Afro-American, Afra American, Colored with a capital C or a small c, and Negro with a capital N or a small n. To be called Black in his generation and in my parents' generation was not a good thing.

To be called Black in his generation was either a cause for a fight with another Black person depending on the complexion of the one doing the name calling; or an absolute throw-down humbug if the person calling an African American "Black" was white!

A major change in the cultural revolution brought about in the late 60s was taking the negative term "Black" and turning it into a positive term. James Brown's "Say it loud! I'm Black and I'm proud!" is musical proof of Dr. Sheares' argument. Tommy Smith and John Carlos' raising their fists in the Black Power salute as the "Star Spangled Banner" was being played in honor of their winning medals during the 1968 Olympics held in Mexico City is Black athletic proof of Dr. Sheares' argument. Blacks were no longer ashamed of being called Black. We became proud of a name, an adjective, and a term that had once been used against us. We turned a negative into a positive. In Biblical language, we "took what man meant for evil" and by the grace of God and the ingenuity of Black genius, turned it around into good. In hip-hop language, we "flipped the script!"

Dr. Sheares argued that the Spanish and Portuguese words *negra*, *negrita*, *negrito* and *negro* all meant black. The untutored European slave traders did not know, could not tell, or did not care whether an African was Ibo, Ibibio, Akan, Yoruba, Ewe, Ga, Hausa, or an African from the Bantu speaking people of southwest, southeast, and southern Africa. To the Europeans they were all "blacks."

Africans were carried into the Caribbean as property. Africans were sold into Central America and South America as property. The trade in African bodies, the commodification of human beings and the heinous act of dehumanization was carried on between each of the European slave traders and buyers in the Western Hemisphere long before reaching the shores of the Thirteen Colonies of Britain. From 1619, however, until 1865 in the incredibly inhuman practice of chattel slavery, from the slave ships' manifests to the bills of sale when referencing Africans all the written or printed materials used the Spanish and Portuguese term "negro" or its derivatives.

Southern whites could not roll the letter "R" as Spanish and Portuguese speakers did when pronouncing the word "negro." Nor did they honor the Spanish and Portuguese pronunciation of the letter "E" which sounds like an "A" to English speakers. Spanish and Portuguese speakers pronounced the word *negro* "naygro" with a rolled "r" but on the tongues of Southern white folks it quickly came to be pronounced "kneegro" or "nigro."

From the English mispronunciation of the Spanish word *"negro"* the word quickly devolved into a negative term "nigra" or "nigger." For almost four hundred years, therefore, the word "negro" was a negative word. That negativity was reinforced in the authorized dictionaries of English speakers until the late 1960s. To be called a "black nigger" was the ultimate slur.

Dr. Sheares argued that this generation of Blacks who were coming of age when King was murdered reached back to the Harlem Renaissance for their cultural understandings of who they were and were therefore, no longer ashamed of being called Black.

Please remember, Dr. Sheares served in Chicago. The headquarters for the Nation of Islam is in Chicago and members of The Nation had been labeled "Black Muslims" by the media for at least a decade before James Brown's song swept the nation.

Doing ministry, therefore, was no longer the same as it was for my parents when it came to the Black Church. Doing ministry with the youth who still attended church was no longer doing ministry with conservative politically respectable Colored folk who did not want to upset the white man. This was an era that was nurtured on the Montgomery Bus Boycott, the sit-ins, the deaths of the civil rights workers, the Southern Christian Leadership Conference (SCLC), the Student Non-Violent Coordinating Committee (SNCC), Stokely Carmichael, Muhammed Ali, Kareem Abdul-Jabbar, Nina Simone's "Mississippi Goddamn!" and a proud Black nation that embraced its blackness; and a generation that was building upon the strong foundations of being Black in a world where the majority of inhabitants on this globe were and are people of color!

Therefore, the first part of this mantra ("unashamedly black") rang true from the soul sounds of Detroit through the "dark ghettos" of Harlem and the Southside of Chicago all the way down to the black bottoms of Louisiana, Alabama, and Mississippi.

Remembering that Chicago was the mecca of the Black Muslims, the home of the Black Hebrew Israelite Nation and the Kemetic Institute, younger Black Christians were in constant arguments with other Blacks their ages who were no longer affiliated with the church. Many Blacks left the church because of its conservative bent. Chicago was also the home of J.H. Jackson, the forever President of the National Baptist Convention, and many Blacks my age questioned Jackson and his ilk whom we considered "Uncle Toms," and we were leaving the Black Church which we saw as a home for conservatives who had no interest in social justice.

It was that large group of Blacks my age who needed ministry, Dr. Sheares argued; and "the old ways" from "back in the day" would not cut it with my generation. The ministry of that Black church required some tweaking and some decolonizing of the theology and the liturgy if the church was to hold young people my age.

He said that he was constantly encountering a group of young Black Christians who were not ashamed to be a Christian. They had Black Muslims in their family. They had friends and loved ones who were a part of the Black Hebrew Israelite Nation. They had wives, husbands and children who claimed Isis, Osiris, and Horus as their deities as they were members of the Kemetic Institute. Many had even embraced the African Traditional Religions and Yoruba Orisha as they gave up on the Black Church.

There was a critical mass of Black Christian believers he had encountered who liked to argue with that group of Muslims, Black Jews, Black Kamites and practitioners of Yoruba religions who called Christianity "the white man's religion." They knew better!

They not only knew better, however, they affirmed loudly that they did not have to apologize for being Christian. Jesus was Black. Moses was Black. The bible took place on the continent of Africa in the Old

Testament from Genesis to Malachi, and they did not apologize for their Christianity. Thus Dr. Sheares' term took on new life: "Unashamedly Black and Unapologetically Christian!"

One half a century later "there arose a new Pharaoh who did not know Joseph." One half a century later, however, the thoughts and feelings of this generation of Black Americans and Black Christians on the continent of Africa have been called into question!

I was asked to lecture at the University of South Africa in 2015. The topic of the conference was "Is Black Theology Still Relevant?" Just as Black Theology took root here in the States, it took even deeper root on the continent of Africa—especially in South Africa.

Dr. Dwight Hopkins' first book, **Black Theology USA/Black Theology USA**, demonstrates this reality. With the first "USA" in Hopkins' carefully chosen title being the United States of America and the second "USA" being the Union of South Africa, he masterfully compares the similarities and differences between the birth and growth of Black Theology on this continent and on the Mother Continent. That was fifty years ago.

Because of desegregation, because of assimilation, because of social media, because of interracial marriages, because of miscegenation, because of mixed race children, because of a generation of Trump followers and because of the intractable nature of White Supremacy, the crazy notion of white superiority and the ignorance of white racists, many African-Americans want to be politically correct and many want to honor the boundaries of political respectability, so their feet "stray from the places," where we met our God. We no longer remember the holiness of the brush arbors. We are now concerned with the high mortgages on our high-rise condos.

Because of the birth of the "Prosperity Gospel" and because of the rebirth of the conservative Black Church which Rafael Warnock describes as us quoting James Cone but channeling Billy Graham, "Black Theology" is being called into question in the early years of the second decade of the 21st Century. The same is true in South Africa when the "new Pharaoh" looks just like us; yet the conditions are worse under the new Pharaoh. A Black face in the White House does not mean a better life for the vast majority of Blacks in the country—America or Praetoria.

To read such a powerful book as Charles Hinsley's collection of essays and poetic affirmations is like a breath of fresh air for me. He has put into words some of the strivings, the longings, the hopes, the love, and the aspiration of millions of Blacks from my age to my grandchildren's age!

Hinsley writes with the ease of a Zora Neal Hurston, the eloquence of a Ralph Ellison and Toni Morrison, the poetic flare of Gwendolyn Brooks, Langston Hughes, and Claude McKay. Some of his works sound just like Langston Hughes' *Jes B. Semple*! Some of his works will have you smiling because of the familiar tone of the barber shop or the beauty salon. Other musings will have you weeping as he draws you into his poetry and his prose which capture the pain and the victory of a "nation within a nation" which still embraces their Blackness and equally embraces their Christian faith.

Hinsley takes you on a journey from Jesus to Jazz. It is a journey you will enjoy. It is a journey that will leave you breathless. It is a journey that will rearrange the furniture in your mental states of being and your mental consciousness; and all I can say to you having read and reread this tremendous work is "Enjoy the journey!"

REV. DR. JEREMIAH A. WRIGHT, JR.
Pastor Emeritus
Trinity United Church of Christ
Chicago, Illinois

ABOUT THE AUTHOR

Charles L. Hinsley was born in Atlanta, Georgia in 1957, but grew up in Asheville, North Carolina from the age of nine months old. He considers Asheville his native home and North Carolina his native state. His early childhood was shaped by a Jim Crow segregated way of life. His all-black community and social lifestyles were distinctively separated from the all-white communities and social lifestyles of his white counterparts. Water fountains that read "Whites Only" clearly distinguished what role in society he was relegated to. And situations, such as having to go into the movie theater through the back door and forced to sit in the balcony, served to reinforce his second-class socially defined place in society. However, his segregated life was drastically punctuated in 1970 when the school system in Asheville integrated. This was a reaction to and a consequence of Dr. Martin Luther King, Jr.'s assassination and murder in 1968 and the social unrest that was raging throughout the nation.

Many clashes between white students and black students took place in Asheville during those turbulent times, and this period had a profound impression upon Hinsley's life, as reflected in his writings. Hinsley graduated from Asheville High School in 1976 and then attended Asheville Buncombe Technical Institute (AB-Tech) the following two years. He then enrolled in Winston-Salem State University, a Historically Black College and University, in 1978 and graduated with honors (Cum Laude) with a bachelor's degree in Psychology in 1982. He attended graduate school in 1983 at Southern Illinois University in Carbondale, Illinois, earning a master's degree in 1991 in Special Education and Correctional Education.

While attending graduate school, he was hired by the Illinois Department of Corrections in 1985 as a correctional counselor and he eventually rose to the rank of Warden. He retired from the IDOC in December 2004. By then, he had worked in every level of our nation's prison system: minimum security, medium security, high-medium security, maximum security, and super-maximum security. He also supervised and managed inmates assigned to death row.

After taking a two-year hiatus, he returned to the workforce. From 2006 through 2007, he worked in the private sector as a Program Administrator for an employment training and job placement agency in Georgia that serviced clients of The Department of Children and Family Services. He subsequently relocated back to North Carolina and was hired by Goodwill Industries of Greensboro in 2008 to be their Program Manager. He designed, implemented, and managed a life skills and employment training program for the Returning Citizen population.

In 2011, he was hired by the North Carolina Department of Corrections in their Community Corrections Division. In this role, he served respectively as a Judicial Services Coordinator and a Judicial Services Specialist responsible for managing offenders that were placed on supervised and unsupervised probation and mandated by the court to complete community service. He and his staff would assign probationers to non-profit agencies and faith-based organizations to perform their court mandated hours and report back to the court their compliance or non-compliance. He worked in this capacity until 2021 when he retired for a second time.

Hinsley's affinity for writing was birthed while attending Winston-Salem State University. Dr. Elwanda Ingram, a black professor of African American Studies, was the person who most influenced his life in this way. Her exposure to him of African American writers, authors, and poets expanded his mind to the wonders of black literature like no one had ever done before. Her passionate love for the works and talents of black writers rubbed off heavily on Hinsley, and he has been trying to continue their phenomenal work of reflecting the unique and varied lifestyles of black folk ever since. This book represents a modest effort of his work.

This is a SPECIAL tribute to one of the greatest Spoken Word poets that I know, and he has blessed me with the honor to share one of his poems.

WATER OUR ROOTS

Let each of us remember
our ancestral roots.
For each one of us
is like a tree
with roots that run real deep.
And there is an ancient promise
that we are supposed to keep,
and that is, to water our roots.

You might say,
How do I water roots
that I cannot see?
How deep do they grow?
How far from the tree?

You find a very special spot,
You make a place of remembrance
for the ancestors you got.
Your great, great, great grandmother
you may not know her name.
But light a candle for that woman
all the same.

And your great, great, great grandfather
you don't know his name.
But tonight, let his spirit see the
light of a flickering flame.

That's how you water your roots.
That goes for you and I,
Because if you don't water your roots
Your tree will die!

— JEAN CLAUDE TORAN —

"Because it had no root it withered away"
—MARK 4:6

THE PREAMBLE

In

the

Beginning

was

the

… WORD …

and the WORD was with GOD

and

the

WORD

was

GOD.

— JOHN 1:1 —

THE PRELUDE

The historical and biblical importance of people of color has never been truthfully represented by those of European descent. The deliberate effort by Western civilization to minimize, discredit, and in many cases, totally conceal the significant role that Africa and persons of African descent have played in world history has had a profound debilitating affect upon the psyche of many persons of color. With the introduction of "racism" as a systematic method of control and oppression against Black people, the truth about our cultural identity as being descendants of kings and queens has been grossly misrepresented and deliberately distorted against us.

The repercussions experienced by African descendants by this omission of historical relevance has caused many people of color not to fully understand their connectedness with their African heritage and subsequently, suffer from not having a real sense of a true identity. But what has been even more catastrophic about the insidious doctrine of racial superiority has been the dehumanizing practice of race-based religiosity. This is the false teachings of European cultures that have espoused that African people, and their descendants were cursed by God for the sins of Noah's son Ham and thus, were not included in the redemptive salvific plan of God. This, of course, is a lie!

The sole purpose of their teaching has been to instill a mindset within us designed to separate African people from the special relationship with God that we know existed from the beginning of the creation of man. For, in God's own words, He decreed, "And the Lord God formed man out of the dust of the ground and breathed into his nostrils the breath of life; and man became a living soul" (Genesis 2:7). The "dust" that God spoke of was the black soil of Mother Africa, the birthplace of all mankind.

So, it is with this knowledge of divine truth and the explicit boldness of God's word that I do not hesitate to proclaim the love for the color of my skin nor shy away from my faith in God. And therefore, I can speak with deep conviction when I say, "I am unashamedly Black and unapologetically Christian." I am not ashamed of who I am as a Black man, and I need not apologize for my belief in Christ Jesus. And as always, God is in control, and He will reveal the rest of me in His own time.

THE IMAGE OF GOD

As a child, it had always been a sense of fascination and wonderment for me what the color of God really was. Although I attended an all-black church and all the people I lived with, played with, went to school with, and socialized with in my childhood were black, I never once saw a black image of God. Not in my church, not in my home, not in my friends' homes— not anywhere. What I did see everywhere was a white, blue-eyed, blonde-haired man that I was conditioned to believe was the one and only image of God. How could that be and why was that so since that "white" God certainly did not look like me? I was in my early teenage years when I grasped the true reason and motivation behind the depiction of why God and Jesus were portrayed as being White. I, being a person of color, was not supposed to have the knowledge nor the power of understanding that me and people who look like me were the chosen people of God. That was not the concept of empowerment for our self-image that our oppressors wanted us to know or even wanted us to remotely conceive as being possible. But I challenge you now to consider these biblical truths.

After the forty days and nights flood that killed all mankind, Noah, his three sons, and their four wives were the only human beings that survived, and they repopulated the earth for all generations thereafter (Genesis 6-11). Noah and his sons were black Africans and therefore, it stands to reason that all who were born of them were black too. Jesus' linage is directly traceable to Noah and his sons through Abraham (Matthew 1). Now consider Hosea 11:1 and Matthew 2:15 where you will find these words," Out of Egypt, I have called my son." This passage is in reference to God leading the Israelites out of Egypt during the Exodus and when Mary and Joseph fled into Egypt with baby Jesus to hide him from being killed by Herod the King.

If Mary, Joseph, and baby Jesus were of "white" skin complexion trying to hide in the black cultural regions of Africa i.e., Ethiopia, Egypt, and Canaan, do you not think that they would have been easily discovered? The reason they were not discovered by Herod's men was twofold. First, because of God's providential protection to ensure Jesus would live to fulfill his purpose on the cross. And second, because Mary, Joseph, and baby Jesus' skin color was the same as the people where they hid, black Africans, so they blended right in. Common sense reasoning should dictate that Jesus was and is undeniably black!

I offer one final point. Here is a short anecdote from James W. Peebles who is the publisher of the African American Study Bible and I quote him from that source. *"One bright, hot southern morning in Nashville, Tennessee, as my sister and I scrambled for rummage over dump heaps, I pulled from underneath a pile of rubbish an old, worn picture of an angel with other small angels flying around her. I said to myself, "Colored angels?" It was a few moments before I could divert my eyes to other rummaging matters, and thinking aloud I kept saying to myself, "There must be colored angels in heaven, too."*

Mr. Pebbles went on to say that many years passed since that discovery, but the image of that colored angel never faded from his memory. And ever since that day, he wanted to help black people see and know that there are colored angels too. I agree with Mr. Pebbles, and I too want black people to see and know that the image of God reflects themselves; black, holy, and beautiful!!

"Don't pray when it rains if you don't pray when the sun shines."

— SATCHEL PAIGE —

CHAPTER ONE

PRIDE

"Negroes everywhere, lift yourselves from the doubts of the past, . . . see things as they are."

— MARCUS GARVEY —

HOMELAND

I sit on the banks of a foreign land wondering of
your ancestry ... your people ... your children

I sit on the banks of a foreign land wondering of
your days ... your nights ... your tomorrows

I sit on the banks of a foreign land wondering of
your springs ... your summers ... your seasons

I sit on the banks of a foreign land wondering of
your dances ... your songs ... your celebrations

I sit on the banks of a foreign land wondering of
your pains ... your tears ... your sorrows

I sit on the banks of a foreign land wondering of
your pride ... your heritage ... your love

I sit on the banks of a foreign land wondering of
your struggles ... your sacrifices ... your oppression

I sit on the banks of a foreign land wondering of
your dreams ... your liberties ... your freedom

I sit on the banks of a foreign land wondering of
the day I will no longer wonder of these things.

The silent and reverent call of Africa

— A day in December 1994 —

AFRICAN AMERICAN BLACK NEGRO CHILD

Who am I ... African American black negro child?
    What am I ... African American black negro child?
        Wherefrom have
            I
              come ... African American black negro child?
Who am I ... I am the voice
    of the
        dream ... Dr. King. What am I ... I am the
messenger
        of
    the legacy ... slavery.
Wherefrom have I come ... I am from the womb
    of
        all civilization ...
            Africa!

Deep within my soul are some questions that I must ask?

— A day in July 1990 —

FREEDOM

It is I who has ownership of my mind, and it is I who has ownership of my body, but it is my Creator who has ownership of my soul. And when I speak of myself it is of those dimensions in which I am speaking. This unification of mind, body, and soul is the essence of my nature and my nature has a natural tendency to act of its own free will. Governed by this innate predisposition to move through life unrestricted and unlimited requires that I generate laws concerning myself that will define and assert my autonomy. However, in the process of employing my efforts to announce my position in the scheme of life and thereby, comply with the freedom that is my nature, I am oftentimes confronted with prejudiced attitudes and inaccurate pictures of myself that are solely designed to disrupt my perception of me being free. But because I faithfully believe in the spirit-filled breath of life that gives power to my soul and liberty to my consciousness, I will attempt to alleviate and repress any, and all such threats against my freedom by whatever method or methods necessary and by all the power vested in me by my Creator. Through a conscious and deliberate effort to ensure my inalienable right to be self-governed and liberated, I will be able to present to others a self that is of the people, by the people, and for the people, but most of all free to be me.

"The right to be free is a truth planted in the heart of men"
—WILLIAM LLOYD GARRISON

Inspired by Malcolm X

— A day in April 1981 —

EQUILIBRIUM

Should I be mad ... damn right! When I read
    about history and they don't even
        attempt to acknowledge me.
I was born with the breath of life from the
    power of the Most High ... How dare they diss me with
some lame-ass alibi?
    Their plan for my life did not include for
me to be free ... so they chose not to
    represent the truth in their version of
        HIS-STORY.
So, should I walk around with my smile turned
    upside down perpetrating a frown,
Hell NO!! Because I refuse to act like some dumb-ass clown ...
    What's up with that?
America, hiding behind the pledge of her democracy,
    perpetrating a fraud with some lady called
        the Statue of Liberty ...
    What is the equilibrium of my American dream?
Injustice ... police brutality ... and every other sort
    of unrighteous thing.
I've made my pledge of allegiance to the United States
    flag of America ... and I'll be damned, if I
still didn't get beat down and dragged with a confederate
        flag.
And I've been told by those good ole boys that I
    should just be thankful to be here ...
because a nigga boy ain't worth the price of a
    coon ... damn buffoon!
So, if this is my plight, then prepare for a fight
    unto the death of me ...
because I'll be damn you see if I let America
    pimp my equality ... So, what is the equilibrium of my
American dream? Being a second-class citizen, life in prison,

and unequal treatment to deny me of what my freedom means... Damn right I'm mad and ready to fight!

The true face of America's claim of freedom and liberty don't represent my best interest of equality!

— *A Day in October 2002* —

FLY IN THE BUTTERMILK

As I looked around the room, it was quite obvious that my pigmentation was distinctively different in color than all the others, and I was the only one... The BLACKNESS of me among the WHITENESS of them, and
    they wanted to keep it a secret, but I was TOO black, for I was the fly in the buttermilk.

But why was I there?
    Was I the Uncle Tom?
        Was I the House Nigga?
            Was I the Shoeshine boy?...
                Surely, some of my colored folks thought so, and surely all of those white folks hoped so...

Hoped so, just so they could feel safe about their separateness from me
    and to be reassured of the myth that WHITE is better than BLACK.
But the color of my skin should have been the least of their worries...
    They should have been worried about the God who put me there,
        for I was the fly in the buttermilk.

"If God be for us who can be against us?"
—ROMANS 8:23

— A Day in November 2002 —

MY POEMS, MY PEOPLE

I write what I feel for no other reason
but to say what's on my mind . . . My poems will
never ever always rhyme, except,
maybe this time!

My people are my people . . . Black folk people, and that's
who I am . . . and I'll be damn
if the world don't
know!

My poems are such that they sometimes don't say
much . . . but my people are my people,
and you better damn well listen to what they
have to say.

What is the message of my poems you might question
with some doubt . . . Could they be of
some speculations, tainted with laden trepidations,
or concealing a hidden revelation . . .
You figure it out!

My people are my people . . . Black folk people
telling the story of all the world's
history and leaving no untruth concealed
about our tumultuous legacy.

My poems have a message all of their own, and
they speak with words often
unknown . . . Spouting out this and saying that
and uttering the sounds of a
labor pain 400 years old!

And my people are my people . . . Black folk people, jazzy,
classy, sassy, and straight up homegrown

down to the bone!
And clever as ever so don't be tricked
by the mere fact that my

house is not in the 'hood . . . 'cause
code switching is what we do to
survive!

I write what I feel for no other reason
but to say what's on my mind . . .

My people are my people . . . Black folk people
and to love them
is what I
do,
. . . and to love them is what I do . . .

HIS-STORY is not a true reflection of our history

— *A Day in September 2002* —

THE DOOR OF NO RETURN

Twenty million souls raped, then aborted from the womb
    of their homeland's protective bosom . . .
made to suffer in the nakedness of their flesh and
    agonizing fears . . . forced to enter the Door
of NO Return, their conquerors disregarded all concerns
    and had no respect for the kings and queens that they were.

Twenty million souls demoralized, then stigmatized for
    the color of their dark skin . . .
deep penetrating scars of languished tormented souls
    of humanity . . . forced to enter the Door
of NO Return, with no chance of going back to the
    sanctity of their homeland and having
to accept the trauma of their ill-fated plight.

Twenty million souls pillaged, then separated from the
    intimacy of their sacred rituals . . .
branded, catalogued, and stockpiled as disposable property . . .
    forced to enter the Door of NO Return,
having been robbed of their freedom as the first
    people of the civilized world
and stripped of their identity as God's chosen people.

Twenty million souls stolen, then enslaved for the prosperous
    economics of their untold labor . . .
the lineage of their ancestors broken by the divide
    of deep ocean waters . . . forced to enter
the Door of NO Return, their righteous heritage was
    purposely defaced which caused them to
bury their songs of pain with those who died
    during the journey.

Twenty million souls imprisoned, then shackled down by
    the life choking grip of inhumanity . . .

incapable of escaping from the suffocating clutch
of a slow death ... forced to enter the
Door of NO Return, their spirit as a great people
died as they saw the shores
of their homeland fade to nothingness.

*The beginning legacy of a stolen civilization
from the coast of Senegal in Africa*

— *A Day in February 2002* —

The "Door of No Return" on Goree Island off the coast of Senegal.

"Many Africans were torn from their families and held as prisoners at this way station before they were shipped off to the new world to be sold as slaves. When I look at this picture, I think of how afraid they must have been."
—CHRIS MILLER

CHAPTER TWO

SPIRITUAL CONSCIOUSNESS

"And the Lord God formed man out of the dust of the ground, and breathed into his nostrils the breath of life; and man became a living soul."

— GENESIS 2:7 —

THE ALPHA AND THE OMEGA

THE LIGHT OF DAY

During the time of eternity past when time's predestined and perpetual existence was sequestered in the womb of infinity, there was complete darkness and life was in a state of permanent hibernation. As life lay motionless and void in the fertility of its celestial habitat, a powerful source of energy intruded upon its bedarkened world and thus, there became light in a once lightless and lifeless existence.

This energy was formed into an illuminating sphere of intense warmth and created an atmosphere conducive for the awakening of a new day. For it is written that God said, "Let there be light; and there was light; and God called the light day; and God made two great lights; the greater light to rule the day." (Genesis 1:3, 5, & 16).

Since the awakening of this new day, mankind's predestined existence has been divinely and innately connected to this magnificent light of life. Thus, mankind's preordained purpose has fostered his growth and has guided his freedom of spirit through countless phases of time. Each phase has intensified man's curiosity to try and understand his existence as it relates to that of the universal order of Divine Creation. For it has also been written that God created male and female in his own image and gave them dominion over every living thing that moveth upon the earth (Genesis 1: 27–28).

Empowered with this supernatural divine authority to govern his world from a position of supreme greatness and be allowed to administer his guidance according to the judgment of his free will, man became enamored with his own glorified status. Thus so, he imprudently and without a discerning sense of fear chose the disobedient and regrettable act of challenging the commandments of his creation. For it is also written that Eve took of the forbidden fruit and did eat, and gave also to her husband Adam, and he did eat (Genesis 3:6).

When Adam and Eve chose this act of blatant disobedience against God's divine law not to eat of the tree of knowledge of good and evil, they instantly separated themselves from His righteousness and summarily condemned themselves from receiving the eternal enjoyment of a perfect and holy existence. They would no longer be innocent and without blemish, for their spiritual souls had now been tarnished by their arrogance of heart and thus, their actions gave birth to mankind's sinful nature.

Thus, the light of day that man had come to know through his manifested divine creation had now been cast out of his perfected soul and placed in the abyss of the conceited darkness of his heart (Genesis 3: 15–24). But being the Omniscient God of the entire universe and possessing the Omnipotent power to bestow unconditional love upon mankind, God provided a way out for man to redeem his soul and still receive eternal salvation.

For it is also written that God so loved the world that he gave his only begotten Son, that whosoever believeth in him should not perish but have everlasting life (John 3:16). Thus, the eternal light of day that mankind had previously come to know through the intake of God's divine breath of life had now been unconditionally restored back to him by way of God's mercy and grace through the birth, life, death, and resurrection of HIS Son, Christ Jesus.

The Lord is my light and my salvation.
—PSALM 27:1

— *A Day in March 2005* —

(THE PARENTHESIS OF LIFE)

Life has but three absolutes: birth, death, and eternity. Herein lies the parenthesis of life, for our complete existence is bracketed within these three terms. To experience this parenthetical transformation, we must transcend from an embryonic state of primitive instincts and thoughtless emotions (our birth) to a state of relative consciousness and human mortality (our life and death) and ultimately to a state of redemption and resurrection (our eternity).

As we transition through the human condition of these dispensations of life, we cannot afford to arrogantly adopt the position that our human manifestation instinctively gives us the exclusive birthright to boldly proclaim our own self-righteousness. For it was this very act of willful disobedience and perverse mockery committed by the first man and woman that established the irreversible covenant that we will surely die (Genesis 2:17 & 3:2).

Having entered into this world with our life already defined by the perfect plan of our Creator's design, the drama of our life is therefore predestined to unfold according to His plan. Thus, by virtue of His eminent grace of life-giving spirituality, the question that we must ask ourselves then becomes "Of what purpose am I?" This question marks the beginning of the challenge that will inevitably confront us all and decisively separate those who have faith from those who have no faith at all. Faith is not an automatic transformation of birth, but rather, a recognition over time of a greater power than ourselves.

However, no matter at what point in our lives the recognition of faith is affirmed, a personal submission to God's omnipotence and a total acceptance of God's sovereignty will be instantly demanded of us if we are to become true faith believers. And then, the dependency of our life on His power and on His power alone and on all that has been created by Him for our spiritual inheritance will reveal itself more clearly. Thus, the answer to our challenging question "Of what purpose am I?" will then become self-evident.

Intrinsic in this axiom between having faith and not having faith is the duplicity of the fact that for those persons who do not reach this recognition of acceptance and thereby develop no faith will have a spiritless life and consequently, their purpose in life will be unfulfilled for they will receive no answer to their question. But for those persons who do recognize the veracity of God's magnanimity, the moment that they comprehend the revelation of His presence in their life they will move from the state of primitive instincts and thoughtless emotions (our birth) to the state of relative consciousness and human mortality (our life and death).

During this transitory state of developing our spiritual awareness and coming into the understanding of the power of our free will and thereby, becoming enlightened to the positional truths of our divine creation, the deluge of unrighteous vulgarities and secular manifestations of prosperity will begin to seductively entice us away from the pathway of spiritual growth and divine prosperity.

It is precisely during this vulnerable time in our transition of discovering the designed purpose of our created existence that we must begin to earnestly strengthen and prepare ourselves spiritually for our day of personal judgment.

No effort of human good, which are those things done for the sake of our own approbation will be acknowledged in the Kingdom of Heaven. Only our efforts of Divine good which are those acts done solely with the intended motivation to do God's will and not the will of ourselves will be approved. As we ready ourselves for life on the other side of human mortality which will represent (our eternity), neither the hour nor the day will be known of our demise. So, what we must do as believers of faith on this side of eternity is to acknowledge the benevolent Omnipotence, the sovereign Omnipresence, and the righteous Omniscience of our Heavenly Creator to ensure our place in eternity future.

And it will be at this point and not before this point that we will become affirmed into the holy sanctum of everlasting to everlasting, and then we will move into our final dispensational state of redemption and resurrection which is eternal life. Thus, the parenthesis of our life will manifest the fullness thereof and come full circle by transcending the dispensations of time and the human conditions of birth, death, and eternity.

The preeminent quality of one's eternal existence will ultimately depend on one's belief in Christ Jesus.

— *A Day in July 2001* —

PERPENDICULAR FOCUS

Our self- perspective of who we are should be perpendicular to and
aligned with the introspective awareness
of our spiritual nature.
Such self-understanding must
filter through from the genesis of life that is
contained within our preordained creation.
Endowed with the ornate power
of divine incarnation, we must recognize that the genesis of our life
embodies the essence of a Holy presence.
Therefore, when we
consider who we are from this point of view,
the recognition of our self will become unmistakably clear
and overwhelmingly dominant in our
self-perception.
Thus, the characteristics of me, myself, and I
will no longer be viewed as "selfish" qualities all unto
themselves, but rather as having a Divine connectedness
with the Trinity of all creation,
GOD THE FATHER, GOD THE SON, and GOD THE HOLY SPIRIT
and therefore, me, myself, and I
will take on the likeness of
being
one
with
HE
as
is
HE
with
me.

One cannot focus on one's "true" self without acknowledgment of God's magnanimity and the one-to-one relationship that exists between us.

— *A Day in July 2001* —

PROOF

Of all the sciences known to man there is but one science that is virtually unchallenged and is universally accepted for its theoretical construct, that being mathematics. Mathematics is considered to be the only "true" hard science because of its propensity to deal in absolutes. Mathematics is the systematic treatment of relationships between numbers and shapes that result in quantitative conclusions expressed by numerical values. However, before I proceed any further in defining the qualities inherent in math, it is important at this point to interject here and offer the impetus for this short treatise.

There are some people in our world society who in all of their vainness have adopted the belief that God does not exist. These persons are known as atheists, and they are unconvinced of the existence of God and His omnipotent being. As such, this simple composition will offer them irrefutable proof of His existence using the concept of mathematics as empirical evidence. Even the atheist understands and accepts the definitive realities of what mathematical truths conclusively demonstrate. So, with that point of clarification stated, I will move forward with my declarative exposition.

In very basic and elementary terms and by employing the concept of mathematics, I submit as a proposition that when you have a quantity of one which represents a positive value and you add to that quantity with another positive value, you will increase the numerical quantity of that one positive value by whatever quantity you add to it. To illustrate this principle in a more definitive and conclusive manner the following example is offered in support.

If you take one apple and you place that apple on a table and you then take another apple and place the second apple beside the first one, you will have increased the quantity of the one apple to a quantity of two apples thus causing a positive numerical outcome and so forth. This is an empirical mathematical truth. Therefore, giving credence to the scientifically based fact that the value of one item plus the addition of another item will inevitably increase the total value of all items involved.

However, from the atheist's point of view, he would not question the outcome; but rather, he would question where did the first apple come from to begin with, because he knows that he cannot intelligently dispute the mathematical truth of now having two apples when he started out with only one.

The response to his cynicism is not profound at all but rather obvious and pragmatic. Simply stated, man himself cannot produce nothing from nothing and end up with something. Or, to state this in a more concrete way using the traditional concept of mathematical principles where 1 + 1 = 2; you typically will not end up with a positive outcome from the derivative of combining two negative values such as -11 minus -4 which will = -7. However, in some rare instances, you can derive the difference of one negative numeric value from another negative numeric value and produce a positive outcome such as -21 minus -36 which will = 15.

But even in a situation such as this where two negative values produce a positive outcome, it is the progression of the larger negative value (-36) advancing toward what is commonly understood to be the positive equilibrium of the numeric continuum as demonstrated by (-3, -2, -1, 0, 1, 2, 3, etc.) that makes the two negative values have a positive outcome and not the mere exclusive fact that both numerical values simply have negative characteristics.

In other words, two negative values can only produce a positive outcome when the combined sum of their total value crosses the common threshold of the *"neutral point of positive progression,"* and based upon the numerical continuum of positive and negative values, the **neutral point of positive progression** is zero (**0**) which for the purpose of this thesis is the metaphorical symbol for divine volition and supreme truth, namely **GOD!**

So, the answer to the atheist's skepticism as to where did the first apple come from to begin with lies in the universal equation of divine law which renders the answer that God created it. Then God said, *"Let the earth bring forth grass, the herb that yields seed, and the fruit that yields fruit according to its kind, whose seed is in itself, on the earth"* and so it was (Genesis 1:11). With that perspective being offered as the prelude to my purported claim of proof, I will now expound on this numerical concept and present the theoretical framework which supports the basis of my mathematical supposition for divine intelligence and thereby, prove the existence of God.

The premise of my theory declares that mankind and all manifestations of life were divinely inspired, were created by a divine intelligence, and that man is incapable of producing the physical manifestation of his own existence from absolute nothingness as only GOD can.

Contrary to my stated premise, the atheist professes that all life is a result of a serendipitous event. They do not believe that there is a celestial power or universal supreme intelligence that created mankind and all therein. And they adamantly argue the position that mankind is a by-product of organisms that have evolved over time. They further claim that through this evolutionary process of organic life, mankind has obtained the innate ability to manifest his own immortality of eternal life through this transformative process.

I submit in refute of their position, that God is God all by Himself and that the magnanimity of His holy existence is the sole source of created life and is the foundation for everlasting eternity. Additionally, I submit that the negative human elements contained in man's sinful nature nullifies the atheist's assertion of self-creation through evolution. For you cannot add a negative human element, such as arrogance with another negative human element, such as avarice, and produce a positive human outcome that will have lasting eternal results. Therefore, the atheist's declaration that man's creation from organic matter through an evolutionary transformation is implausible because man's core nature is imperfect, and perfection cannot be produced from an imperfect source, except by way of divine intervention and divine authority.

If you were to apply the atheist's theory of evolutionary organic creation to the theory of social evolution, you would quickly learn the fallacy of their argument. The general definition of social evolution is defined as mankind's effort to continually strive to reach a higher level of self-actualization for the purpose of achieving a utopian state of existence. The resulting outcome of achieving such a prominent state of social order could not be obtained without the cosmic influence of a divine source. Man, in and of himself, is too flawed to obtain such perfection. Thus, one must concede that the foundational basis of all life begins at the **neutral point of positive progression**, God!

The **neutral point of positive progression** for individuals who humble themselves to the undisputable reality of their human existence lies in their unselfish and genuine acceptance of a higher power greater than themselves. However, in the mind of an atheist, a higher power greater than himself does not exist and as such, they view themselves as their own neutrality of life. This arrogant attitude is a negative characteristic that cannot produce an everlasting eternal positive outcome. Such characteristics align themselves on the negative spectrum of the human creation continuum as illustrated by the following analogy:

Atheism				*Christianity*		
-3	-2	-1	0	1	2	3
conceit	arrogance	narcissism	(GOD)	faith	truth	righteousness

Thus, based upon this mathematical numeric principle the only logical conclusion that one can render from accepting the atheist's paradigm of evolutionary organic creation is that human society could never reach an optimal place of utopian existence because there will always be individuals who will insist on rejecting the reality of mankind's existence as being contributable to something greater than himself. Therefore, the sum total of an atheist's negative human characteristics could never add up to where they would cross the spiritual threshold of the **neutral point of positive progression** because that would require "faith" and faith is a prerequisite for the acceptance of God's existence and an atheist harbors no faith beyond himself.

The atheist is too conceited in their self-centered belief to allow faith to be given any credence that God exist. They are content to maintain their benign belief that they and only they, have the power to determine their own eternal fate. Notwithstanding their cynicism, in order for an atheist to advance beyond the **neutral point of positive progression**, they must accept the irrefutable reality of their own existence and acknowledge that all life emanates from a source greater than themselves.

The point of this mathematical presentation is to demonstrate through a universally accepted form of science that man's existence could not have come into being based solely upon the serendipitous circumstance of chance as the atheist boldly professes that it had to have occurred. In the realm of mathematical systems, the element of "chance" is entirely dependent upon the presence of an existing variable that gives substance to its potential numerical probability. In other words, any probable set of conditions that come into existence must have a neutral starting point by which each variable can be accounted for and thus, be factored into the formulary equation of possible outcomes.

So, for an atheist to simply say that God does not exist, and that the existence of mankind is merely a by-product of organic life, he does not account for the most critical variable in the universal equation of life and that being OMNIPOTENCE! Without this variable factored into the universal equation of creation which represents the neutral starting point of all life, the probability that mankind came into existence as a by-product of organic life merely by "chance" would then have some credibility. But because the variable of "omnipotence" **cannot** be excluded from the equation, this makes the atheist's position of chance render a zero-sum plausibility.

So, based upon this mathematical position, I subscribe to the precept that all life, human and non-human, share a common denominator predicated upon a universal divine law whereby God created the heaven and the earth and all thereof in six days (Genesis 1:1–25). The common denominator of this universal equation is the equilibrium value of the **neutral point of positive progression**, God!

Additionally, it is my assertion that the creation of mankind is also based upon the mathematical principle of divine law whereby the human DNA formulary of the X/Y chromosomes (male/female) plus the spiritual DNA formulary of the B/L chromosomes (breath of life) equals CREATION! Mankind does not have the inherent ability to produce the mathematical value of the B/L chromosomes and therefore, he cannot create life from nothingness, only God can!

Consequently, man's existence could not have come into being based upon the haphazardness of chance or the negative characteristics manifested from his self-centered nature because the synthesis of man's ego is formulated by a flawed disposition characterized by deceit, falsehood, and imperfection, qualities which have no lasting eternal power. But to the contrary, the universal law of divine creation which is formulated from an equation constructed using supernatural intelligence always produces outcomes that have everlasting power for all eternity. So, no matter how much an atheist believes or argues that he controls his own fate, the true reality is that his existence is not based upon an evolutionary process of micro-organisms coalescing together over time to create his reality of flesh and bones. But it is simply that he too was created by God and his eternal existence is also dependent upon God's chosen fate for his life whether he accepts this truth or not.

In conclusion and contrary to the assertion by the atheist that God does not exist, man's existence, inclusive of the atheist's existence, is the qualitative proof and quantitative summation of a singular divine universal mathematical equation which renders the formula: positive volition (+) truth (+) creation (+) humanity (=) **GOD!** The mathematical and divine empirical evidence of **HIS** omnipotent existence.

— You do the math —

Positive Volition—*The prevailing quality and benevolent grace of God's will.*

Truth—*The irrefutable and self-evident quality of fact.*

Creation—*The manifestation of nothingness into living flesh by divine authority.*

Humanity—*The shared condition of all mankind.*

God—*The Alpha and the Omega and sustainer of all life.*

— A Day in October 2001 —

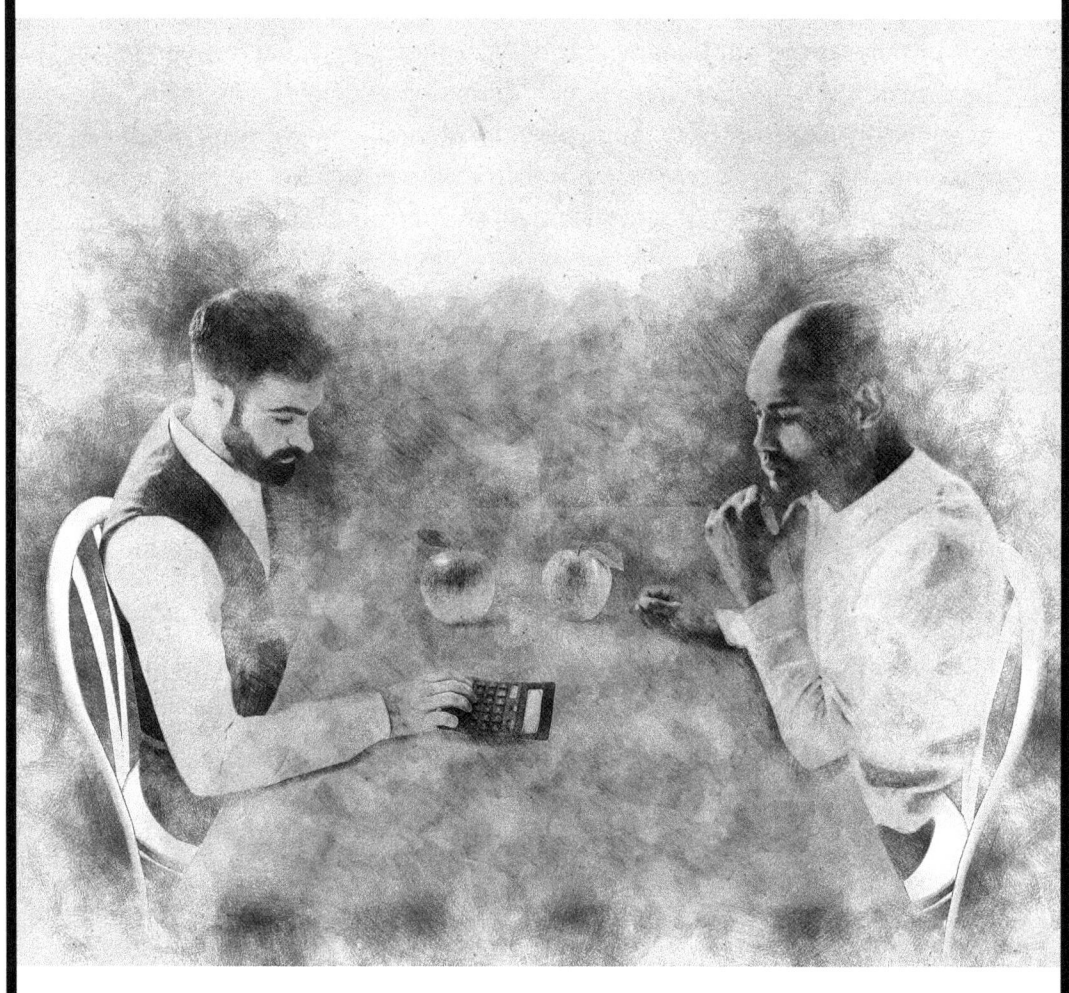

DIVINE PROCLAMATION

Of what account is the world's fertile soil if there is no measure of righteousness for which freedom can give birth to the inherent liberties of human life? For it was conceived in the mind of the Universal Creator that TRUTH and MAN would forever be linked together. Thus so, during the creation of eternity past it became man's innate birthright to rightly seek the truths of life from the very moment life was breathed into his nostrils and man became a living soul. And it was at that precise moment in time and with that singular act of Omnipotence that all men were created equal.

Preempted with a natural inclination of having a free will, every unselfish human act that is manifested by mankind is a positive form of self-expression intended for the purpose of acquiring spiritual emancipation. But to become fully emancipated man must experience various degrees of trials and tribulations that will test the character of his spiritual resolve. Therefore, any action that man genuinely ascribes to be a proclamation of his spiritual freedom and declares as his solemn right to determine his own actions of free will, he must also be prepared to submit to the virtue of supreme humility by yielding to the manifest will of God. In other words, is mankind truly capable of loving his neighbor and washing his feet?

This, then, becomes man's individual freedom of choice for which all men possess and for which all men must unashamedly proclaim if the virtues of divine righteousness associated with the inherent liberties of our human nature are to prevail on earth. However, when man chooses to protest against the natural inclinations of his moral compass and does so without regard of the evidence of life's prevailing truth, but instead, does so with a self-serving nature that completely disregards the sovereign covenant of his spiritual birthright, his emancipation will cease to be, and he will become a menace unto himself and a slave unto his own self-righteous conceit.

The intrinsic duplicity of man's free will to accept or reject God's sovereignty will inevitably provoke inner conflict. Consequently, this conflict will cause man's conscious enslavement of his conceit to declare a spiritual civil war between truth and falsehood. Truth, being the virtuous and absolute characteristic representative of man's positive volition toward God and falsehood, being the unrighteous and conceited characteristic representative of man's negative volition toward God will induce a diametrically opposed state of spiritual consciousness; good versus evil.

To achieve eternal peace between the revolt of man's fallen self (evil) versus that of his obedience to God (good), man must surrender in total humility to God's absolute deity and only then will the proclamation of his spiritual emancipation have the chance to enjoy the bounty of divine prosperity for all eternity.

> *". . . and ye shall know the truth and the truth shall set you free . . ."*
> —JOHN 8:32

— A Day in November 2001 —

CHAPTER THREE

NEGRO TALK

"I have always thanked God for making me a man, but Martin Delany always thanked God for making him a Black man."

— FREDERICK DOUGLAS —

COTTON CLUB SISTER

She walked into the club very classy and very bold,
Her presence altered the ambience, and the drama began to unfold.
She was known around town as Lady Sweet Sugar "C,"
She was sophisticated and elegant, but also a bit sassy.
She had a very smooth style and moved with a sensual grace,
The look in her eyes captivated every person in the place.
Styling her physique in a tight black satin dress,
The crowd all knew Lady "C" was about to stir up some mess!
She strolled to her table in a slow uptown walk,
The sister's game was tight, and her game caused much talk.
She sat down at her table and ordered herself a drink,
She looked at the bandmaster and gave him an enticing wink.
The band started jammin' and the club began to throw down,
But Lady "C" just sat there real cool and grooved to the soulful sounds.
She sat there for a while just scoping out the scene,
Just watching every motion and sizing up everything.
Her conversation was reserved, and no one would dare speak,
Her game was most serious, and she always played for keeps.
She then got up and walked over to Cool Papa Joe,
Without saying a word, she grabbed his arm and took him to the dance floor.
Cool Papa Joe could handle his own and was pretty smooth on his feet,
But, when Lady "C" started doing the hoochie, Papa Joe couldn't compete.
She grabbed another brother and began to twirl him around,
She then started doing what was called, the Cotton Club Get Down!
She worked her body in all kinds of gyrations and moves,
The rhythm of the music made her body feel the power of the groove.
She danced all night until the last beat was played,
Then, she strutted out the club as if the Queen of the Mardi Gras parade.

They called her Lady Sweet Sugar "C"

— *A Day in March 2002* —

A STREET CORNER CHESS GAME

"It's your move, chump" . . .
"Don't rush me, nigga, I'll move when I get good and ready, punk!" . . .
"Hold up on that noise man, you best give a brother some respect" . . .
"Respect?" . . . "You can't even spell 'respect' dumb ass fool" . . .
"Who you callin' a fool?"
"I ain't talkin' to myself so I must be talkin' to you!" . . .
"Man, the only fool around here is your silly ass" . . .
"Tweedle-dee, tweedle-dumb, look out world, here comes Willie
   lump, lump!"
"Man, you talk cash shit, are you ever gonna move or just talk out the
   side of your neck all day?" . . .
"Whatever I decide to do, your clown ass cain't and ain't gonna do a
   damn thang about it" . . .
"Will somebody come get this chump before his mouth overload his
   lil' narrow ass?" . . .
"Ain't nobody gotta come get nobody but you, 'cause if you can't
   stand the heat get your punk ass off the street!" . . .
"Man, you're full of shit, I don't even know why I bother putting up
   with your jive ass" . . .
"I'll tell you why; 'Cause nobody else but me will listen to that
   nonsense that you be talkin'" . . .
"Oh, it's like that now, you feelin' sorry for a brother?" . . .
"Hell nah! . . . I just like laughing at your dumb ass" . . .
"Move chump!" . . .
"Check mate!!!" . . .
"Well, I'll be damn!" . . .
"You see fool, you study long you won't go wrong, so now take your
   chump ass home
      . . . next!"

The brother got schooled!

— A Day in January 2002 —

BROTHER RAY

Brother Ray, why you so cool?
    ...Could it be that you understand the legacy of the
blues?
    And I know that you know what it feels like
to be down and out...not a dime
    in your pocket and no food in
        your mouth!
Brother Ray, some people try to say that your
    coolness ain't cool at all...
But they don't seem to understand your story of the
    chain and ball.
    Doing time, hard time brother Ray on
the chain gang, but it was your street way that
    earned you your ghetto
    Hall-of-Fame...And I understand, so brother Ray
don't be ashamed because I know you still got
    some straight up homegrown game
    left to play...But it ain't just
about the game homeboy, it's about the blues
    down deep in your soul where the
    birth of the cool begins to unfold.
Movin' and groovin'...jivin' and divin'...slippin' and dippin'
    and sometimes straight up ego trippin'...
    Watch out homeboy because it's all a part
of the life of your struggle and strife.
    So, brother Ray it's cool to be cool when
you've learned the lesson of the blues
    from the school of hard knocks...
...but you best remember that you are the standard
    by which these young jitterbugs sell
their rocks and not care that they too, might
    get locked up!
So, tell me brother Ray, why you so cool?
    Are you the joker, the jester,

or the ghetto fool? The blues have been
        around for all your life,
but you don't seem to think twice before you
        roll the dice.
The game of life is a serious matter
and a game you certainly don't
        want to lose,
So, brother Ray, you best remember that
        your "coolness" came from the birth of the home
down blues, I'm outta here ... Peace!

Cool brother Ray is the street teacher for survival in the 'hood.

— A Day in January 2003 —

SISTER 'TRISH

"Sister Trish, why you twist the way you do?"

"Are you trying to make a brother fall in love with you?"

"Well of course I am Brother Cool, that's what I do!"

"Well, stroll your fine ass over here and let me spit a little rap on you!"

"Brother Cool your words better be clever as ever 'cause
my love ain't for play and I damn sho' ain't gonna waste my time of day
for whatever!"

"So, Sister Trish, you think you got game, huh?"
"Then lend me your earhole for a brief minute and you'll
know that I can come straight up with it!"

"Brother Cool, don't play me for no fool 'cause I'll have your
jive ass playing hooky from school."

"I got you Sister Trish and my words will make you wish
that you could handle my shit!"

"My game is tight Brother Cool and you don't have a damn clue
of the love game played by ghetto rules."

"Maybe I don't homegirl, but I'm still willing to play in your world."

"Then play at your own risk 'cause in the end you'll learn
that you can't handle the force of my twist!"

"Well, I'll be damn, I just been schooled!"
"Momma told me about girls like this cool, sweet, sexy Sister Trish.

Brother Cool got played by a street walker

— A Day in February 2003 —

BAY-BAY KIDS AND NEGROES

Junebug ran out the house almost knocking
    the screen door off its hinges . . .
Bay-Bay screamed at him like she was the police . . .
    "Stop running in my house boy before
you break sumpin' and then I'll have to break yo'
    little ass!" Junebug got outside
where it was safe because he knew a fight
    was about to get started. He saw Bay-Bay's
boyfriend, "Skeet" coming over to the house
    and he was drunk . . . Bay-Bay had
li'l baby in her arms while the other kids
    were fighting and carrying on
in the back room. "Hey baby! I just came over
    to get me some of yo' good lovin' . . .
Give yo' man a kiss." "Nigga, get yo' bad breath
    smelling ass outta my face and
sit your drunk ass down!" "Baby, why you gotta
    talk to me like that?" "'Cause you's
drunk nigga, and you ain't gonna be laying
    up with me smelling like some
dead ass skunk. "Woman, every time I have a li'l
    drink you start trippin'," . . . I
wouldn't be trippin' if you knew how to hold
    yo' liquor." "Forget that bullshit
woman . . . whatta ya' got to eat?" "So now
    you want me to feed yo' drunk ass
too, huh? "Well hell yeah, since you ain't
    gonna give me no snatch, I might
as well eat sumpin'." "You know, you are a
    downright pitiful ass fool, boy!"
"Woman, would you just fix me a damn plate and quit
    runnin' off at the mouth?"
"Damn it, Squeaky! What the hell have ya'll
    done broke now? Get the hell

outta my house before I beat the damn shit
      outta all ya'll. Who the hell is knocking
at my door? What's up, Skeet? I saw you pull
      up man so I came over to see if you
got my money." "Nah, Bossman, I ain't holding' on
      to nuttin' right now." "Nigga!
you been saying that shit for three weeks,
      when you gone pay me, man?"
"Hey look, Bossman, I'll have a li'l sumpin' sumpin'
      next Friday. Can I tighten you up
then?" "Yeah, that's cool, man . . . "You got any beer
      in this house?" "Hey Bay-Bay!
get Bossman a beer and bring me one, too!"

Niggas and flies, Niggas and flies, and the more
I see Niggas, the more I like flies.

— A Day in July 2003 —

NIGGA STREET

The time was 1967, the same year I came
    upon the age eleven . . . and it
was on that day that I trembled, and it was
    on that day that my momma cried
when she told me about a man shot dead
    on a street called Southside.
The man called him a "Nigga!" on the street
    where he lay . . . The people all
stood back with fear and had nothing to say.
    It was over the numbers, illegal
as they were, but on Nigga Street the
    numbers came before the meat.
A father was now dead with his children left
    behind . . . another father was sent to
prison for murder and a lifetime. Food on
    our tables and clothes on our backs,
the numbers helped pay the bills for folks
    on my side of the tracks.
Each day was a new day and life and death
    would often meet because on
Nigga Street the numbers always came
    before the meat.

A day in the life of Black folks in 1967

— A Day in July 1993 —

NINE-ELEVEN, 2001

Black folks have been terrorized for over

    400 years ... Rapes, lynchings, burnings,

beatings, and senseless killings.

    Now America you know what it feels like

        ... and ...

    I'm safer in the 'hood than you are

in the White House ... don't run

    scared now!

From the perspective of a ghetto black man

— A Day in October 2001 —

[Update: The threat has now come home to roost—Jan. 6, 2021]
... and 20 years later the perspective is still the same,
"Now America you know what it feels like", but this time
it's because of people who look just like YOU!

— A Day in April 2022 —

CHAPTER FOUR

NOTIONS OF LIFE

"The best blood in my veins is African blood, and I am not ashamed of it."

— FRANCES ELLEN WATKINS HARPER —

WHERE THERE'S A WILL, THERE'S A WAY

She would be so tired when she came home with the
weight of the whole world pressing
her down, down to the ground,
and I was too young to understand
it all...
But she would gather all her strength just so
she could raise her kids up right...
The sacrifices she made will go unaccounted for by the world,
but nonetheless are immeasurable
in my life. Her strength came
from God's eternal
omnipotent
light.
And when the hard times would come, she would always say in a calm
reassuring
voice,
"Where there's a will, there's a way."
I
understand that
now!
She was a proud woman and oh so, very wise in her years...
teaching us by example of living for the Lord.
The uncertainties of life did not seem to bother her,
and I often wondered, "What was her secret?"...
because I was too young to understand it all.
She wept sometimes,
but would always say, it would be okay.
Then, I would hear her pray in her soft humble voice,
"Where there's a will, there's a way."
I
understand that
now!

Flesh of my flesh...bone of my bone...I crawled from my mother's womb.

— *A Day in October 2002* —

INTIMATIONS OF THE ESSENTIALS

When the gray tentacles of change come forth in the late season of time
gradually replacing the youthful innocence of our life,
longevity has been mercifully kind,
sharing of her wisdom through much sacrifice.

Should we not gladly cherish life's dearest secrets
when whispered to us in private?
Holding on to precious remembrances like the plumbs of an egret,
Treasuring essential advice from the voice of mother wit.

As does the bell toll with each warning note,
causing the quietness within us to stir ...
Our arrogance then dies and cannot gloat
And we tremble with fear in silent murmur.

Perhaps not considering the consequences of our actions
while plotting for a course of lifelong success,
Forgetting the principles of the order of creation,
we become marred by the trials of life's elusive happiness.

Relationships beckon for love's intimate embrace,
the winds of change make love unstable ...
Love has but one omniscient face,
where there is a will God is able.

Fundamental to the natural order of all things
life meanders through the hills and valleys of our hopes.
Searching desperately to find what truth really means,
Is it eternal life after death unprovoked?

Confronted by lifeless stares from faceless people,
Having no identity of their rites of heritage.
Descendants unknown and scattered abroad through ageless seasons,
knowing our spiritual lineage is the key to life's rites of passage.

Foreboding as life oftentimes can be,
shadowing the hidden truths of her meaning...
Faith provides the elixir and lasting remedy
for those questions in life that are misleading.

We are momentary imprints within the vast realm of the universe,
Our mortality has a finite plan and a divine purpose.
There are reasons for our miraculous creation of human birth
of which the blood of Christ Jesus was the purchase.

Destined by circumstances that are unknown to us
and prayerfully responding to the laden dramas of life,
Our existence first came from the dust and
there we shall return hoping to escape from our vice.

Searching endlessly abound for life's expressed gratitude,
Mistakenly believing that she owes us an apology.
We ourselves are the ones who have been rude,
needing to make amends before she recites our eulogy.

When the dawn of life fades beyond our horizon,
may our living measure up to its potential.
The many things of life that were an abrasion,
were necessary lessons for intimations of the essentials.

*Listen closely for the echoes of grace and mercy
and the whispers of God's love.*

— A Day in July 2003 —

SPEAK TO MY HEART

You called my name oh Heavenly Father before
the dawn of life came to past
and my reply was but a whisper.

You announced your presence to me as I was in
the womb of creation
and my reply was but a whisper.

You spoke to me with the gentle voice of grace
that only your love can command
and my reply was but a whisper.

You commanded my existence through the miracle
birth of my soul
and my reply was but a whisper.

You herald my name among the heavens on high
that I am your child
and my reply was but a whisper.

You proclaimed my name in the Book of Eternal Life
with the resurrection of Christ Jesus
and I whispered
I
believe!

God hears the softest of whispers spoken from your heart.

— A Day in July 2001 —

COLLATERAL IMPACT

Nations at war and under siege by the tyrannical
thirst for power. It's indeed a **dark, dark** hour in our present-day history.
Devastation, repudiation, insurrection ... all signs of maladaptive
infestation of fanatically obsessed immorality.

Damage control is "Out-of-Control" and on the run,
And we can't seem to stop the gun from shooting its victim,
rat-a-tat-tat-tat-tat!!!
The world's compassion has grown numb from the senseless killings of
innocent people,
and the strain inflicted upon her brain has caused the world to go
TOTALLY, TOTALLY INSANE!!!
(There are not enough strait jackets to go around)
You oppress me,
    you persecute me,
        you arrest me,
            you imprison me,
                you execute me,
                    you bury me ...
The collateral impact is all the same,
murder begets murder as does **self-destruction** begets **annihilation**!

The life and times of the Book of Revelation

— A Day in November 2002 —

TO BE

In the stratosphere of lingering moments long before eternity past had
announced itself to the dawn of life,
the soul of our being was present in the womb of creation . . .

When the emptiness of nothingness prevailed upon
the immensity of time's perpetual existence and the vast realm of
infinity extended far beyond the boundaries
of her celestial horizons,
the soul of our being was present in the womb of creation . . .

As time came into the knowledge of its own
existence wondering about the meaning of its celestial
manifestation. Having been conceived from the
fertile sperm of Omnipotence, time became impregnated with
the immaculate conception of life and thus,
the soul of our being was present in the womb of creation . . .

Light years before the awakening of the first
moment of destiny, the inherent nature of our purpose was divinely
imputed into us and our unique essence of spirituality
was affirmed by the Heavens on High.
Thus, the soul of our being was present in the womb of creation . . .

And, at the instant moment of our beginning
when the "Word" became flesh the Universal Creator said,
"Let there be life!"
Thus, my child, you have become destined to be!

*"Before I formed thee in the belly, I knew thee, and before thou camest
forth out of the womb, I sanctified thee, and I ordained thee."*
—JEREMIAH 1:5

— A Day in November 2003 —

THOUGHT COLLECTOR

Wondering about what makes me wonder about
    the ideas that I think about
intrigues me to be curious about what
    thought will come next even
though the notion about pondering a situation
    may not cause a spontaneous
reflection of moments of self-awareness but
    does inspire me to meditate about
my spirituality deeply contemplating the reality
    of my existence and being totally
mindful of the intellectual energy that it
    takes to understand the definitive
conclusion of my vision of life and when the
    cognitive hypothesis of my philosophy
does not render an empirical fact then the
    metaphorical symbols transform
into the abstract context of my imagination
    and the inclination to deliberate
about the symbolisms of my existence stimulates
    the ideas that are dormant in
the recesses of my cerebral intuition thus
    given rise to the instinctive
nature of all that I am to be manifested in
    the flesh and thus, a dormant
thought begets an idea and an idea begets
    words of expression.

"In the beginning was the Word"
—JOHN 1:1

— *A Day in November 2002* —

TEARS OF THE SON

    Resistant to instruction,
            rebellious against correction,
                    and unwilling to accept spiritual direction.
Of what manner of immorality has man's life become?
    The vanity of his selfishness has chosen not to run
        from the wickedness of his volition,
but his soul still cries out for tears of the son.

    In the brightness of day, the translucent light of power shines
        down on all mankind, but lurking in the shadows of the
darkness of his heart is the deceitfulness of his hatred. Carrying the
    seed of deception in the loins of his old sin nature
and repudiating every divine purpose to be God's Holy Creation,
      the vanity of man's selfishness will only produce an apocalyptic
        outcome,
          but his soul still cries out for tears of the son.

    Undaunted by the vengeance of God's mighty wrath
and defiant against the power of HIS redemptive resurrection. Displaying
    absolute rejection of God's magnanimity for HIS righteous
omnipotent deity, the warfare against God's healing restoration has
    sinisterly begun and the vanity of man's selfishness has cast
out the light of truth and God's holy face has been shunned,
    but his soul still cries out for tears of the son.

      Contemptuous toward humility,
            confrontive against righteous morality,
                  and not believing in divine spirituality,
Of what manner of indignity has man's life become?
    The vanity of his selfishness speaks with false pride and evil tongue,
But glory be to God, man's soul can still receive mercy from tears of the son.

"For what shall it profit a man, if he shall gain the
whole world and lose his own soul?"
—MARK 8:36

— *A Day in February 2003* —

CHAPTER FIVE

SILHOUETTE SOLILOQUY, A JAZZ FINALE

Jazz takes all the elements of our culture and puts them into perspective.

— BILLY TAYLOR —

MISTY BLUE

The sound of her voice imitated the softness
    of the melodies of spring...
and was reminiscent of a sweet melodic tempo
    that could soothe your soul.
The vibrant discords of her enchanting sound
    seemed to float effortlessly in
mid-air as they playfully danced to the
    tune of a hummingbird's
song. The intricate patterns of her lyrical
    expressions resonated magically
from the depths of her inner soul, exposing
    her sensitivities about life
and expressing her secret passions about love.
    Her voice was scintillating and
descriptive of a romantic love story accentuated
    by subtle intonations of
spontaneous emotions. She serenaded my heart
    with style and charisma
and interjected into my mind the vision
    and clarity of the rhythms of life.
The creativity of her expressive language would
    make you feel the serenity of absolute
peace and harmony with all things around you. And, as
    the movements of life revealed the meaning
of her words, the sound of her voice seemed misty blue.

A Trumpet's Serenade

— A Day in May 2003 —

MISTY BLUE

When in love, flatter your heart with jazz!

CONTEMPLATION OF JAZZ

Melodies of the heart must first come from the soul!

INCANDESCENT SOUND

Created with an African soul,
    she was born
        in a cotton
            field ... separated from her people
and her first song was of them.

Heavy chains,
    a loud moan,
        and tribal drums were the spiritual essence that formed
            her identity.

        Syncopated rhythms of impetuous melodic sounds
            expressed her brazen
                attitude,
                      and the troubled days of her life
that were etched ever so vividly in her face spoke of the
    pain inside,
        but the melody in her soul
    permitted her spirit to soar free ...

Then, "Satchmo" came along and gave her love
    and her face smiled forever!

        ... JAZZ ...

*Louis "Satchmo" Armstrong made love to the sounds of life and
helped create the most beautiful sound in the world, Jazz!*

— A Day in October 2001 —

MY MUSICAL HERITAGE

This is a 1949 photograph of my dad and his jazz band. His name was James Jay Hinsley, II, and he lived in Atlanta, Georgia where I was born. He was a brilliant mathematician and math teacher from what I have been told. He and his band used to play on what is known as the Chitlin' Circuit. A collection of cities and small towns situated along the eastern part of the United States from Florida to New York and parts of the Midwest. It was called the Chitlin' Circuit because many of the club owners sold chitlins and other soul food dishes out of their kitchens to the patrons of the club as well as to the various bands that performed there. I never knew my dad because he and my mom separated when I was only nine months old, and he was never in my life after that. But glory be to God, I learned to forgive him, and time moved on, and so did I. I believe that I inherited my affinity for jazz music from him, and I pray that he is in Heaven smiling down upon me!

He is in the center of the picture playing the saxophone

SOLO PERFORMANCE

"I believe there is a place that lives within us all. It's a place of vision and clarity where the rhythm of life moves in harmony with a higher consciousness. The purpose of jazz music is to take you there. So, as in music, so as in life".
—JIMMY SOMMERS, JAZZ MUSICIAN

www.ingramcontent.com/pod-product-compliance
Lightning Source LLC
Chambersburg PA
CBHW050634150426

42811CB00052B/803